WHITE STAR LINE

Royal Mail Triple-Screw Steamers

"OLYMPIC" AND "TITANIC."

Built and Engined by Harland & Wolff, Ltd., Belfast.

The Liverpool Printing & Stationery Co. Ltd.,

Mercer Court, Redcross Street.

White Star Liners " OLYMPIC " and " TITANIC."

THE advent of these Leviathans of the Atlantic coincides very appropriately with the most important development of modern times—the movement of the British and American people towards the ideal of international and universal peace. Of all the forces contributing to this great and desirable consummation, commerce has been one of the most potent, and as the growth of international trade is largely due to the progress in shipping, it is impossible to over-estimate the service rendered to the Anglo-Saxon race by the enterprise of our Shipowners and Shipbuilders. No better instance of this spirit of enterprise can be produced than the building of the White Star Liner "Olympic" and her sister ship "Titanic," constructed as they have been side by side at Messrs. Harland & Wolff's Ship Yard, Belfast. The spectacle of these two enormous vessels on adjoining slips, representing over 100,000 tons displacement, was altogether unprecedented, and naturally the public interest taken in the vessels on both sides of the Atlantic has been very keen. It has been felt that, great as the triumphs have been in the past in Naval Architecture and Marine Engineering, these two vessels represent a higher level of attainment than had hitherto been reached; that they are in fact

A. Vertical Keel Plate and Floors looking Forward.

B. Vessel more than half Framed.

C. "Olympic" and "Titanic" on Stocks.

4

D. Bow View on the Stocks.

in a class by themselves, and mark a new epoch in the conquest of the Ocean, being not only much larger than any vessels previously constructed, but also embodying the latest developments in modern propulsion.

For convenience the description of the vessels has been arranged in three parts—the first dealing principally with the hull, the second with the decorations, and Part III. with the machinery,

I, The construction and general features of the ship. Leading Dimensions:—

Length over all	882' 9''
Length between perpendiculars	850' 0''
Breadth, extreme	92' 6''
Depth, moulded, keel to top of beam, bridge deck...	73' 6''
Total height from keel to navigating bridge	104' 0''
Gross tonnage	about 45,000 tons.
Load draft	34' 6''
Displacement	about 60,000 tons.
Indicated horse-power of reciprocating engines	30.000
Shaft horse-power of turbine engine	16,000
Speed ... ... ·	21 knots.

The various views given herein illustrate the construction of both vessels and their machinery.

The work of both ships has been carried on in a most expeditious manner. The first keel-plate of the "Olympic" was laid on December 16, 1908, and by March 10 following the double bottom was all bolted up, and the work of riveting it by hydraulic power well advanced. The whole of the side framing, which was commenced from the stern, was finished by November 20, 1909, and the plating was completed and almost entirely riveted by April 15, 1910. The vessel, as is well known, was launched 20th October, 1910, and practically only seven months have been taken up in the subsequent work of completion. When the dimensions of the ship are remembered, this performance will be recognised as highly creditable to all concerned.

The view of the "Olympic" on page 4 shows two months' progress. There is seen the centre keelson, which is 5' 3" deep, and under it the flat keel-plate 1½" thick, with the keel bar below 3" thick, while projecting on each side are the tank floor-plates, ready for the first of the intercostal girders, which extend right fore and aft. There are four such girders on each side between the centre keelson and the margin plate, but under the machinery compartments there are additional girders. Between the margin plate and the turn of the bilge are wing ballast tanks. In Fig. B the margin plate is seen to the left, with the wing tanks in course of construction. The whole of the double bottom thus built up was riveted by hydraulic power, the machines, as shown in Fig. A, being suspended from the overhead travellers. The double bottom is utilised for carrying water ballast, the floor plates between the intercostal girders having lightening holes, except at intervals, where they are without holes, to form separate ballast-tanks.

Fig. B shows three and a half months' progress. The frames extend to the bridge-deck— the eighth level from the inner bottom—a height from the bilge of 66 feet, and are spaced three feet apart, except at the bow and stern, where they are respectively 24 in. and 27 in. apart. They are of channel section, 10 in. deep amidships, and of angle and reverse bars at the ends. At frequent intervals there are heavy-web frames. Increased strength is ensured at the machinery spaces by the web-frames being placed at closer intervals. Specially heavy bracket plates connect the frames with the wing brackets.

As the framing proceeded the transverse beams were fitted in place on each deck-level. These beams are made of channels 10 in. deep, up to the lower deck, and of smaller section above this: all are placed, of course, to suit the spacing of the frames, to which they are connected by efficient brackets. There are four longitudinal girders in the width of the hull extending for the whole length of the ship. These are built up of plates with deep angles at top and bottom. Owing to the width of the holds required for the machinery spaces, these girders could not be made continuous; but at the engine and turbine compartments special girders were put in with a collective sectional area equal to that of the four girders in other parts of the ship. Stanchions are erected at frequent intervals under the girders; those under the middle deck—the third level above the inner bottom—are of built-up steel columns, and above this they are of solid steel of less diameter. The latter section was adopted, as they could be placed at more frequent intervals. On the lines of these girders and columns the deck-plate has been increased in thickness. This general description of the structure indicates the great strength of the hull, the aim being to ensure the maximum of stiffness in a heavy sea-way. To the same end the deck plating, which is of steel throughout, was specially strengthened by having thicker plating on the two topmost levels of the moulded structure—on the shelter and bridge-decks.

The shell-plating also is exceptionally heavy. It is for the most part of plates six feet wide and of about 30 feet in length. The width tapers towards the ends, as shown in the bow and stern views of the completed ship. The laps are treble riveted, and the sheer-strakes in the way of the shelter and boat-decks have been hydraulically riveted. This also applies to the turn of the bilge, where bilge-keels, 25in. deep, are fitted for 295 feet of the length of the vessel amidships.

There are fifteen transverse water-tight bulkheads, extending from the double bottom to the upper deck, at the forward end of the ship, and to the saloon deck at the after end—in both instances far above the load water line. The room in which the reciprocating engines are placed is the largest of the water-tight compartments, being about 69 feet long; while the turbine room is 57 feet long. The boiler rooms are generally 57 feet long, with the exception of that nearest the reciprocating engine compartment. The holds are 50 feet long. Any two compartments may be flooded without in any way involving the safety of the ship.

The two decks forming the superstructure of the ship and the navigating bridge are built to ensure a high degree of rigidity. At the sides they are supported on built-up frames, in line with the hull-frames, but at wider intervals. The deck-houses are specially stiffened by channel-section steel fitted in the framework, and where, as on the boat-deck, the public rooms pierce the deck, heavy brackets are introduced to increase strength against racking stresses when the ship is steaming through a heavy sea-way.

Expansion joints are made in the superstructure above the bridge-deck at convenient points in the length—one forward and one aft—the whole structure being completely severed and the joints suitably covered.

Stern-Frame and Boss-Arms.

The stern-frame of such a vessel is of special interest. It was made by the Darlington Forge Company, and some idea of its size may be formed by the fact that the total weight of the casting was about 190 tons, the stern frame being 70 tons, the side propeller brackets 73¼ tons, and the forward boss-arms 45 tons. A view of the stern castings is given in Fig. D, page 10.

A

Rudder.

C

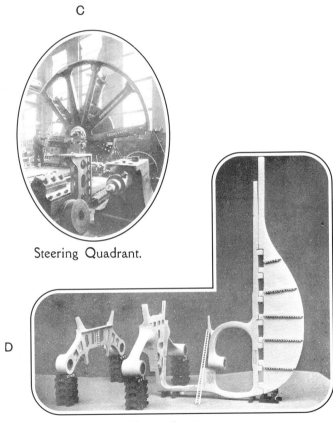

Steering Quadrant.

B

Rudder Head.

D

Stern Castings.

The centre propeller, driven by the turbine, works in the usual stern-frame aperture, while the wing propellers are supported in brackets.   The chief dimensions of the stern castings are as follows :—

Stern-frame :

Height	67' $0\frac{1}{2}$"
Length of keel-post	37' 4"
Section of gudgeon-post	21" $\times$ 13"

After brackets :

Centres of shafts	38' $10\frac{3}{4}$"
Diameter of bosses	5' $2\frac{1}{4}$"

Forward brackets :

Centres of shafts	38' $5\frac{1}{8}$"
Diameter of bosses	6' 2"

The stern-frame is of Siemens-Martin mild cast steel, of hollow or dish section, in two pieces, with large scarphs, one on the forward post and one on the after post, connected with best Lowmoor iron rivets, 2" in diameter, the total weight of rivets being over a ton.   The care exercised in fitting these to ensure a strong connection is suggested by the fact that they were all turned and fitted and specially closed with rams.   There are in all 59 rivets in the forward and 53 rivets in the after scarphs.   In the stern-frame there is, of course, the boss for

Watertight Doors.

the shaft driven by the turbine, the lower portion of this part of the stern-frame having a large palm cast on its extreme forward end, to give a solid connection to the after boss-arms and main structure of the vessel.

The after boss-arms are also of mild cast-steel, of hollow section. Particular attention was paid to the angle of these boss-arms, to ensure the easiest flow of stream-lines to the turbine propeller, in order that it might rotate in solid water. The boss-arms are in two pieces, connected at the centre line of the vessel by strong, deep flanges, to form a continuous web across the ship. This web, again, is riveted to a 2″ steel plate of special quality forming a bulkhead across the ship. Forward of this boss there is another set of arms of the girder pattern, the port and starboard pieces being connected again in the centre of the ship; and, in addition, there are other heavy web-plates down the ship's side connecting same to the ship's floor.

The Rudder.

The rudder, which is illustrated on page 10, was also constructed by the Darlington Forge Company Limited, and is of the usual elliptical type, of solid cast steel, built in five sections, coupled together with bolts varying from $3\frac{1}{2}″$ to 2″ in diameter. The top section of the rudder is of forged steel from a special ingot of the same quality as naval gun-jackets. On the completion of the forging an inspection hole was bored through the stock of the rudder, in order to ensure that there were no flaws. The rudder-stock is shown in a lathe, with the core slung alongside, on page 10. The rudder pintles are arranged each to take its own proportion of the rudder weight, having hard-steel tops or cups inside the stern-post gudgeons. The pintles are 11″ in diameter, of hard steel, and are fitted with a taper in the rudder gudgeons so that they can be tightened up in the gudgeon when required. These are provided on top with a solid covered nut having set-pins to prevent the pintles turning. A special feature is that the bottom of the rudder is so arranged that screw jacks can be employed for lifting it in dry dock. This will greatly facilitate this work. The total weight of the rudder is 101¼ tons, while its length over all is 78′ 8″, and its width 15′ 3″. The diameter of the rudder-stock is 23½″

The Stem.

The stem is of the usual rectangular section, of rolled steel with a cast-steel forefoot of hollow section connecting stem to keel plate and keel bar. A special feature is that there is provided at the top a hawse-pipe, and through this a steel wire hawser can be passed for use in connection with a central bower anchor, in addition to the port and starboard anchors. The centre bower anchor is of 15½ tons weight, and the side anchors are each 8 tons in weight, the cables used, 330 fathoms long, being of 3⅜″ diameter. The centre bower anchor has a wire rope instead of a cable, the length of the rope being 175 fathoms, the breaking strain being 290 tons. The innovation of a central hawse-pipe had the great advantage that it reduced the necessary weight of the side anchors to reasonable limits.

A. Vessel Entering Dry Dock.
B. Vessel Entering Water,
C. One of the Funnels alongside Vessel.
D, Lifting in Boilers.

15

Dining Saloon.

The Arrangement of the Decks.

There are ten decks in the ship, named from the bottom upwards:—Lower orlop, orlop, lower, middle, upper, saloon, shelter, bridge, promenade, and boat. The passenger decks— promenade, bridge, shelter, saloon, upper, middle, and lower, are named alphabetically A, B, C, D, E, F, G. Two of the decks are above the moulded structure of the ship. The lower orlop, orlop, and lower decks do not extend for the complete length of the structure, being interrupted for the machinery accommodation. The bridge deck extends for a length of 550 feet amidships, the forecastle and poop on the same level being respectively 128 feet and 106 feet long. The promenade and boat decks are also over 500 feet long.

The first class passengers are accommodated on the five levels from the upper to the promenade decks. The second class passengers have their accommodation on the middle, upper and saloon decks, and the third class passengers on the lower deck, forward and aft, and on the middle, upper and saloon decks aft.

Passenger Accommodation.

For first class passengers there are 30 suite-rooms on the bridge deck and 39 on the shelter deck. These are so arranged that they can be let in groups to form suites, including bedrooms, with baths, &c., with communicating doors. But on each of these two decks, close to the companion-ways, on either side, adjacent rooms are fitted up as sitting or dining-room.

In all there are nearly 350 first class rooms, 100 of these being single berth rooms. There is accommodation for over 750 first class passengers.

For second class passengers the rooms are arranged as two or four-berth rooms, the total number of second class passengers being over 550. For the third class passengers there is a large number of enclosed berths, there being 84 two-berth rooms. The total number of third class passengers provided for is over 1,100.

The arrangement of the passenger accommodation has been very carefully worked out. There is a first class main companion-way at the forward end of the accommodation, extending from the boat-deck to the upper-deck, with large halls on each level, while further aft is a second companion-way extending from the promenade deck to the shelter deck. There are two second class companion-ways,—one extending from the boat deck to the middle deck, and the other from the bridge deck to the middle deck, the second class public rooms being placed between them—viz., the smoke room on the bridge deck, the library on the shelter deck, and the dining saloon on the saloon deck, with the staterooms on the saloon, upper, and middle decks. There are three elevators incorporated in the main companion-way for the first class passengers, and one in the main second class companion-way for the second class passengers. The first class elevators extend from the upper deck to the promenade deck, with entrances at each deck level. The second class elevator extends from the middle deck to the boat deck.

On the boat deck accommodation is provided for the captain and officers, containing smoke-room and mess-room. Rooms for the Marconi installation are also arranged in the same house, with the wheel-house and navigating bridge adjoining at the fore end. The first class main companion-way ending on this deck has a handsome dome overhead in a spacious entrance, and adjoining this entrance is a large gymnasium fitted out with the latest appliances

First Class Promenades.

The first class promenades on the three top decks in the ships are exceptionally fine. The bridge deck (B deck) promenade is entirely enclosed. It is a magnificent space over 400 feet long, 13 feet minimum width each side of the vessel, and with a solid side screen fitted with the large square lowering windows that constitute one of the most popular features of recent passenger vessels. These windows can be raised or lowered at will, and thus passengers can enjoy the conditions they prefer, having protection from the weather, and at the same time an uninterrupted view of the horizon.

The deck above this, the promenade (or A) deck, is the principal promenade, and is entirely devoted to first class passengers. It is more than 500 feet long and forms a splendid promenade, the width in parts exceeding 30 feet. This is covered by the deck above, but is open at the sides above the bulwark and rail.

The topmost deck—the boat deck—also devoted to first-class promenading, is 200 feet long and the full width of the ship. This deck is surmounted only by the open canopy of heaven.

Reception Room.

20

Disposition of Rooms, &c.

On the promenade deck forward are a large number of the single-berth rooms for first class passengers, the reading and writing room, 41' 0" × 41' 0", with the lounge adjoining, 59' 0" × 63' 0", and further aft the first-class smoke room, 65' 0" × 61' 0", with a verandah palm court built in two compartments, each 30' 0' × 25' 0". The bridge deck is devoted very largely to single-berth and suite rooms, with à la carte Restaurant, 60' 0" × 45' 0".

On the shelter deck there are a great number of first class staterooms and suites, special dining saloons for maids and valets, Marconi and postal officials, and offices in the entrance hall, and, abaft of amidships, the second class library 58' 0" × 40' 0". The third class smoke-room and general room are under the poop on this level.

The saloon deck, as its name suggests, is largely occupied by the dining rooms. Abaft of the grand stairway is a reception room the full width of the ship and 54 feet long, leading into the dining saloon, which is also the full width of the ship and 114 feet long, having seating accommodation for 532. The pantries and galleys are abaft this, and then the second class dining-room, which also is the full width of the ship, is 71 feet long, and has seating accommodation for 394.

First-class staterooms are at the forward end of the main first class companion-way, and are arranged to accommodate one, two or three passengers. The second class staterooms are situated immediately abaft the second class dining saloon, and further aft are the third class staterooms.

Accommodation is provided on the upper deck for first class passengers on the starboard side, in one, two and three-berth rooms, the accommodation for the stewards and restaurant staff being fitted on the port side off the working passage. Second and third class staterooms are also provided on this deck.

On the middle deck is situated the third class dining saloon amidships, extending the full width of the ship, and for a length of 100 feet, with seating accommodation for 473 passengers; the third class galley, pantries, &c., adjoining. At the forward end, convenient to the first class main companion-way, are arranged the Turkish baths, including steam, hot, temperate, cooling and shampooing rooms. Convenient to these are situated two electric bathrooms and also a commodious swimming bath. Staterooms for second class passengers are arranged for on this deck aft, as well as third class passengers both forward and aft.

Another innovation on board this ship is the provision of a squash racquet court. The court is situated on the lower deck, and extends two decks high for a length of 30 feet. A spectator gallery is placed at the after end of the court on the middle deck level.

Excellent accommodation for the firemen has been provided at the forward end of the vessel, through the lower, middle, upper and saloon decks, giving access to the boiler rooms by two spiral stairs and tunnel. The arrangement keeps the firemen entirely clear of the passenger accommodation.

The engineers' quarters are on the middle deck, and the mess room, pantries, offices, &c., on the deck above—off the working passage.

The post office and baggage accommodation is arranged compactly in the forward end of the vessel, with the view of expediting the reception and despatch of the mails on the departure and arrival of the ship.

The Steering Gear.

The steering gear fitted on the shelter deck is, as can readily be imagined, very massive, the diameter of the rudder-stock—23½in.—affording some idea of the dimensions. The gear is of Harland & Wolff's wheel-and-pinion type, working through a spring quadrant on the rudder head, with two independent engines having triple cylinders, one on each side. Either engine suffices for the working of the gear, the other being a stand-by. A view of the quadrant in the lathe is given on page 10. It is so designed as to minimise the shocks received in a sea-way. The spur and bevel gear is of cast steel. The gear is controlled from the navigating bridge by telemotors, and from the docking-bridge aft by mechanical means. In general design the gear resembles that which has given so much satisfaction in all recent White Star ships. The steering gear of a ship is rightly regarded as of the highest importance, and Harland & Wolff's gear has long been recognised as constituting an element in the safety of the vessels in which it is fitted.

Restaurant.

The Anchor Gear.

We have already referred to the anchors, and to the additional centre-anchor on page 14. The latter involved an addition to the usual design of windlass gear, which in these, as in other large liners, is by Messrs. Napier Brothers Limited, Glasgow, and has proved by the test of time to be very reliable. In addition to working the windlass, one of the two engines fitted drives through worm gear a large drum at the forward end and opposite the central aperture on the stem. This drum is grooved to take the wire rope of the centre 15-ton anchor, adopted instead of the more usual cable. Clutch-engaging and brake gear has been fitted, and every detail embodied to ensure the satisfactory working of the cables under all conditions.

A strongly-built crane is fitted at the centre line of the forecastle deck for handling the 15-ton anchor, which is placed in a well in the deck immediately abaft the stem.

The capstan gear, operated by steam engines, is also by Messrs. Napier, and includes on the forecastle two capstans worked by the windlass-engines, two with independent engines, and on a lower level one for handling mooring-ropes. Aft there are five capstans, with four steam-engines, one of which actuates two capstans.

Navigating Appliances.

The navigating appliances are most complete. In addition to the two compasses on the captain's bridge and one on the docking bridge aft, there is a standard compass on an isolated brass-work platform in the centre of the ship, at a height of 12 feet above all iron-work and

Main Staircase.

78 feet above the water-line. Adjacent to the bridge there are two electrically-driven sounding-machines, arranged with spars to enable soundings to be taken when the ship is going at a good speed. All observations can thus be taken under the direct control of the officer in command. The telegraphs are by Messrs. J. W. Ray & Co., of Liverpool, and communicate with engine-room, capstan and other stations. As already indicated, there is also telemotor gear for the steering of the ship. The vessels are fitted with complete installation for receiving sub-marine signals.

The lifeboats, which are 30 feet long, are mounted on special davits on the boat-deck.

The ship has two masts, 205 feet above the average draft-line, a height necessary to take the Marconi aerial wires, and to ensure that these will be at least 50 feet above the top of the funnels, and thus clear of the funnel gases. The masts are also utilised for working the cargo by means of cargo spans, and in addition there is on the foremast a derrick for lifting motor-cars, which latter will be accommodated in one of the foreholds.

Cargo Cranes.

There are three cargo hatches forward and three aft. Two of the forward hatches are served by steam winches, the gins being fixed to cargo spans, while the third hatch—that nearest the passengers' quarters—is served by two Stothert and Pitt electric cranes, designed to lift 50 cwt. They have a radius of 27 ft., a height from the deck to the centre of the pulley

Lounge,

of 29 ft., and a total lift of 100 ft. The hoisting motors fitted are of 40 brake horse-power, and the slewing motors 5 brake horse-power.

All the hatches in the after part of the ship are served by electric cranes of the same make; two of these are on the promenade deck, there being two small hatches to the hold below, so as to form a minimum of interference with the promenading space. The cranes here are of 30 cwt. capacity, the radius being 21 ft. The height between deck and pulley is 20 ft., while the total lift is 80 ft. In this case the hoisting motors are of 30 brake horse-power, and the slewing motors of 3 brake horse-power. For the remaining two hatches aft there are four electric cranes of 50 cwt. capacity, corresponding exactly with those already referred to, except as regards the radius, which is, in the case of two cranes, 28 ft., and of the other two, 29 ft. The height to the centre of the pulley is, however, slightly less than the forward cranes, being 27 ft. and 26 ft. respectively.

The lifting speed at full load is 160 ft. per minute in the case of the 50-cwt. cranes, and 200 ft. in the case of the 30-cwt. cranes, and increases automatically at lighter loads, whilst the slewing speed in all cases is 500 ft. per minute.

In addition to the electric cranes, there are four 3-ton electric cargo winches at the hatches, operating through gins on the cargo spans; also four 15-cwt. electric boat and baggage winches.

Smoke Room.

Electrically Controlled Watertight Doors.

The watertight doors in a vessel of this size are, of course, a most important item, and the illustrations given of some of these doors will doubtless prove interesting. Those giving communication between the various boiler rooms and engine rooms are arranged, as is usual in White Star steamers, on the drop system. They are of Harland & Wolff's special design, of massive construction, and provided with oil cataracts governing the closing speed. Each door is held in the open position by a suitable friction clutch, which can be instantly released by means of a powerful electric magnet controlled from the Captain's bridge, so that, in the event of accident, or at any time when it may be considered advisable, the Captain can, by simply moving an electric switch, instantly close the doors throughout, practically making the vessel unsinkable. In addition to the foregoing, each door can also be immediately closed from below by operating a releasing lever fitted in connection with the friction clutch. Moreover, as a further precaution, floats are provided beneath the floor level, which, in the event of water accidentally entering any of the compartments, automatically lift and thereby close the doors opening into that compartment if they have not already been dropped by those in charge of the vessel.

A ladder or escape is provided in each boiler-room, engine-room, and similar watertight compartment, in order that the closing of the doors at any time shall not imprison the men working therein; though the risk of this eventuality is lessened by electric bells placed in the vicinity of each door, which ring prior to their closing, and thus give warning to those below.

II.—The Decorations.

It is impossible to adequately describe the decorations in the passenger accommodation; the ship must be seen and inspected for these features to be fully appreciated. They are on a scale of unprecedented magnificence; nothing like them has ever appeared before on the ocean. The following brief description of some of the principal rooms, together with the illustrations, will convey some idea of the artistic treatment and luxurious appointment.

First Class Dining Saloon.

This immense room has been decorated in a style peculiarly English—that, in fact, which was evolved by the eminent architects of early Jacobean times. It differs from most of the great halls of that period, chiefly in being painted white instead of the sombre oak which the 16th and 17th century builders would have used.

For details, the splendid decorations at Hatfield, Haddon Hall, and other contemporary great houses have been carefully studied, the coved and richly-moulded ceilings being particularly characteristic of the plasterers' art of that time.

The furniture of oak is designed to harmonize with its surroundings, and at the same time to avoid the austere disregard for comfort in which our forefathers evidently found no hindrance to the enjoyment of a meal.

Five hundred and thirty-two passengers can dine here at the same time; but as we saunter round the room between the groups of chairs, we see that the semi-privacy of small parties has been carefully provided for: we come to several recessed bays in which families or friends can dine together practically alone, retired from the busy hum of surrounding conversation.

Reception Room.

Dignity and simplicity are the characteristics of the reception room. Its beautifully-proportioned white panelling in the Jacobean style, delicately carved in low relief, will indeed make a fitting background to what will probably be the most brilliant *mise-en-scene* on the ship, for it is here that the Saloon passengers will foregather for that important moment upon an ocean-going ship—*l'heure ou l'on dine*—to regale each other with their day's experiences in the racquet court, the gymnasium, the card-room, or the Turkish bath.

The handsome bronze ceiling lights, or the wall-brackets, will reflect their hundred lights upon the glittering jewels of women in brilliant evening frocks, and the black coats and white fronts of the men gathered round the room. Some of the passengers will stand to gaze at the magnificent tapestry directly facing the staircase, specially woven on the looms at Aubusson, or will await their friends seated upon the capacious Chesterfields or grandfather chairs upholstered in a floral pattern of wool damask, or the comfortable cane furniture distributed at intervals.

B. Verandah Café.　　　　　　　　**A.** Turkish Bath Cooling Room.

Upon a dark, richly coloured carpet, which will further emphasize the delicacy and refinement of the panelling and act as a foil to the light dresses of the ladies, this company will assemble—the apotheosis, surely, of ocean-going luxury and comfort. What more appropriate setting than this dignified Jacobean room redolent of the time when the Pilgrim Fathers set forth from Plymouth on their rude bark to brave the perils of the deep!

Restaurant.

The Restaurant is of the Louis XVI. period in design, and is panelled from floor to ceiling in beautifully marked French walnut of a delicate light fawn brown colour, the mouldings and ornaments being richly carved and gilded. In the centre of the large panels hang electric light brackets, cast and finely chased in brass and gilt and holding candle lamps. On the right of the entrance is a counter with a marble top of fleur de pêche, supported by panelling and pilasters recalling the design of the wall panels.

The room is well lighted by large bay windows, which are a distinctive and novel feature, and give a feeling of spaciousness. These are draped with plain fawn silk curtains with flowered borders and pelmets richly embroidered. The windows themselves are divided into squares by ornamented metal bars. Every small detail, down to the fastenings and hinges, has been carried out with regard to purity of style.

Sitting Room of Parlour Suite *(Louis XIV.)*

The ceiling is of plaster, with delicately modelled flowers in bas relief, forming a simple design of trellis in the centre and garlands in the bays. At various well-selected points hang clusters of lights ornamented with chased metal gilt and crystals.

The floor is covered with a rich pile carpet of Axminster make, and a non-obtrusive design of the period in a delicate vieux rose, which forms an admirable background, and completes the harmonious ensemble,

Comfort has been well considered in the arrangement of the room. It is furnished with small tables, to accommodate from two to eight persons, with crystal standard lamps and rose-coloured shades to illuminate each table.

The chairs have been particularly well studied, and are made in similar light French walnut to the walls, carved and finished with a waxed surface and upholstered with an interesting tapestry representing a treillage of roses in quiet tones assisting the general harmony of colour.

For convenience of service there are several dumb-waiters encircling the columns and forming part of the decorative scheme.

On one side is ample accommodation for an orchestra, partly recessed and raised on a platform, flanked on either side with a carved buffet, the top part being a vitrine to hold the silver service, and the lower part for cutlery, thus completing the necessities for a well-appointed restaurant to satisfy every requirement.

Bedroom of Parlour Suite *(Adams.)*

Staircases and Entrances.

We leave the deck and pass through one of the doors which admit us to the interior of the vessel, and, as if by magic, we at once lose the feeling that we are on board a ship, and seem instead to be entering the hall of some great house on shore. Dignified and simple oak panelling covers the walls, enriched in a few places by a bit of elaborate carved work, reminiscent of the days when Grinling Gibbon collaborated with his great contemporary, Wren.

In the middle of the hall rises a gracefully curving staircase, its balustrade supported by light scroll work of iron with occasional touches of bronze, in the form of flowers and foliage. Above all a great dome of iron and glass throws a flood of light down the stairway, and on the landing beneath it a great carved panel gives its note of richness to the otherwise plain and massive construction of the wall. The panel contains a clock, on either side of which is a female figure, the whole symbolizing Honour and Glory crowning Time. Looking over the balustrade, we see the stairs descending to many floors below, and on turning aside we find we may be spared the labour of mounting or descending by entering one of the smoothly-gliding elevators which bear us quickly to any other of the numerous floors of the ship we may wish to visit.

The staircase is one of the principal features of the ship, and will be greatly admired as being without doubt the finest piece of workmanship of its kind afloat.

Lounge.

The lounge, being a room dedicated to reading, conversation, cards, tea-drinking and other social usages, is decorated in the style which was in vogue in France when Louis XV. was on the throne, when social intercourse was the finest of fine arts, and when the Salon was the arena in which the keenest intellects of the age "crossed swords" and exchanged the most delicate conversational thrust and parry.

Now, as then, the British workman is supreme in the production of the finely-carved "boiseries" with which the walls are covered, and in which, without interfering with the symmetry of the whole, the fancy of the carver has everywhere shown itself in ever-varying details.

When talk becomes monotonous, we may here indulge in bridge and whist, or retire with our book or our letters to one of the many quiet retreats which reveal themselves to the thoughtful explorer. The chairs and sofas are so soft and cosy, however, that on them inducements to slumber may easily prevail, to the detriment of our literary efforts.

Smoke Room and Verandah.

The walls are panelled with the finest mahogany, carved in the taste of our Georgian forefathers, and relieved everywhere with inlaid work in mother-o'-pearl.

Here, seated around the home-like fire, we may enjoy Mr. Norman Wilkinson's fine painting of the Approach to the New World, and meanwhile smoke and drink as wisely and well as we feel inclined.

The light comes tempered and softened through the painted windows, where the voyager sees depicted the ports and beauty spots with which he is familiar or hopes to visit, as well as some of the gay and glorious ships which in the past wore so beautiful an aspect, with their low prows and soaring sterncastles.

Here, too, are personifications of the Arts—Poetry, Painting, and the like--which have adorned our surroundings and ministered to our pleasures.

Passing through the silently-revolving doors, we emerge upon a gay little verandah, over whose green trellis grow climbing plants, which foster the illusion that we are still on the fair, firm earth; but one glance through the windows, with their beautifully-chased bronze framing, adds to the charm, and we realize that we are still surrounded by the restless sea, once so dreaded a barrier to national intercourse. Set in this flowery arbour are numerous inviting little tables, at which we can take our coffee or absinthe in the open air, much as we do in our own summery gardens on land.

Bedroom of Parlour Suite *(Georgian.)*

42

The Cooling Room.

The cooling room on the middle deck in connection with the Turkish baths is in many respects one of the most interesting and striking rooms on the ship. The port-holes are concealed by an elaborately-carved Cairo curtain, through which the light fitfully reveals "something of the grandeur of the mysterious East."

The walls are completely tiled, from the dado to the cornice, in large panels of blue and green, surrounded by a broad band of tiles in a bolder and deeper hue.

The dado and doors and panelling are in a warm-coloured teak, which makes a perfect setting to the gorgeous effect of the tiles and the ceiling, the cornice and beams of which are gilt, and the intervening panels picked out in dull red. From these panels are suspended bronze Arab lamps. The stanchions are cased also in teak, carved all over with an intricate Moorish pattern, surmounted by a carved cap.

Over the doors are small gilt domes, semi-circular in plan, with their soffits carved in a low-relief geometrical pattern.

As those who partake of Turkish baths are constrained to spend a considerable time in the cooling room, no pains have been spared to make it interesting and comfortable.

Around the walls are low couches, and between each an inlaid Damascus table, upon which one may place one's coffee, cigarettes or books.

A. Gymnasium.   B. Swimming Bath.   C. Squash Racquet Court.

As the drinking of fresh water is one of the concomitant features of the benefits of taking the bath, there is a handsome marble drinking fountain set in a frame of tiles. There is also a teak dressing table and mirror with all its accessories, and a locker to which valuables may be committed, whilst scattered around the room are innumerable canvas chairs.

Reading and Writing Room.

The pure white walls and the light and elegant furniture show us that this is essentially a ladies' room.

Through the great bow window, which almost fills one side of the room, we look out past the deck on which our companions in travel are taking the air, over the vast expanse of sea and sky.

An atmosphere of refined retirement pervades the apartment; a homely fire burns in the cheerful grate; our feet move noiselessly over the thick, velvety carpet, and an arched opening leads to an inner recess—a sanctuary so very peaceful that here it would seem as if any conversation above a whisper would be sacrilege.

First Class Staterooms.

The finish and decoration of the first class staterooms are well in keeping with the excellence of the public rooms; the staterooms are also exceptionally large and beautifully furnished.

Second Class Dining Room

Perhaps the most striking are the suite rooms. of which there is an unusually large number, decorated in different styles and periods, including the following :—Louis Seize, Empire, Adams, Italian Renaissance, Louis Quinze, Louis Quatorze. Georgian, Regence. Queen Anne, Modern Dutch, Old Dutch.

Each of the first class staterooms has a cot bed in brass, mahogany, or oak, and in most of the suite rooms the cot beds are 4 feet wide. This is a distinct feature which will be greatly appreciated by passengers.

SECOND CLASS ACCOMMODATION.

The White Star Line has done much to increase the attractions of second class accommodation during recent years, having made a special feature of this in a number of their vessels; and in the "Olympic" and "Titanic" it will be found that this class of passenger has been very generously provided for. It would have been difficult, a few years ago, to conceive such sumptuous appointments in the second class. Nothing has been omitted in the determination to place the two new White Star leviathans beyond criticism as to the excellence of the accommodation both in the second and third classes.

The Second Class Dining Saloon is situated on the saloon deck aft: it extends the full breadth of the vessel, and is an exceedingly fine room, with extra-large opening pivoted sidelights arranged in pairs. The panelling of this room is carried out in oak, the design of which

Second Class Promenade Deck.

Second Class Smoke Room.

Second Class Stateroom.

is taken from examples in the early part of the 17th century, with details of a somewhat later period introduced. There is a handsome sideboard extending the full length of the after bulkhead, surmounted with cabinets elaborately carved. At the forward end a specially-designed sideboard, with piano in the centre, is provided; the furniture is in mahogany, the upholstery of crimson leather, and the floor has linoleum tiles of special design.

The Second Class Library is another excellent apartment, with panelling in sycamore handsomely relieved with carvings; the dado is in mahogany and also the furniture, which is of special design, covered with tapestry. A large bookcase at the forward end, the windows at the sides, of large dimensions, arranged in pairs, draped with silk curtains, and the handsome Wilton carpet complete the general comfortable—indeed, luxurious—appearance of the room.

Second Class Smoke Room.—In this room the decoration is a variation of Louis XVI. period; the panelling and dado are of oak relieved with carving; the furniture is of oak of special design, covered with plain, dark green morocco; the floor is laid with linoleum tiles of special design.

The Second Class Forward Entrance and Staircase is handsomely carried out in oak. This staircase is one of the features of the ship, as it extends through seven decks, and an elevator incorporated with the centre of the staircase serves six decks.

The Second Class After Entrance and Staircase is also panelled in oak and extends through five decks.

Third Class Reading Room.

Second Class State Rooms.—The majority of these rooms are arranged on the well-known tandem principle, ensuring natural light to each cabin; the rooms are finished enamel white, and have mahogany furniture covered with moquette, and linoleum tiles on the floor.

Second Class Promenade.—Needless to say, the spaces provided for second class promenades in this vessel are unusually spacious, and the enclosed promenade is a unique feature which will be fully appreciated by passengers.

THIRD CLASS ACCOMMODATION.

The accommodation for third class passengers in these steamers is also of a very superior character, the public rooms being large, airy apartments, suitably furnished, and in excellent positions, and the same applies to the third class staterooms and berths.

The Third Class Dining Saloon is situated amidships on the middle deck, consisting of two saloons extending from ship's side to ship's side, well lighted with sidelights, and all finished enamel white; the chairs are of special design. The position of this apartment—i.e., in the centre of the ship—illustrates the wonderful strides made in passenger accommodation in modern times. Third class passengers to-day have greater comfort on the ocean than first class passengers had before the great developments had taken place for which the White Star Line is largely responsible.

The Third Class Smoke Room is situated aft on the shelter deck. It is panelled and framed in oak with teak furniture, and is a very suitable and comfortable room. Here, under the soothing influence of the fragrant weed, many a thought will be given to the homeland and those left behind.

Third Class General Room.—This is also aft on the shelter deck. It is panelled and framed in pine and finished enamel white, with furniture of teak. This, as its name implies, will be the general rendezvous of the third class passengers—men, women and children— and will doubtless prove one of the liveliest rooms in the ship. The friendly intercourse, mutual helpfulness and bonhomie of third class passengers is proverbial, and, remembering that many of them have arrived at the most eventful stage in their career, we realize that "touch of nature that makes the whole world kin." The new field of endeavour is looked forward to with hope and confidence, and in these vessels the interval between the old life and the new is spent under the happiest possible conditions; in fact, were Mark Tapley on the "Olympic" and "Titanic," he would find these conditions all too favourable for his fellow-passengers to need the display of his exceptional qualities.

Third Class Promenade.—To add, as it were, the finishing touch to the excellent provision made for the comfort and well-being of the third class passengers, there is a large apartment arranged under the forecastle as a third class promenade, and fitted with tables and seats, so as to be useful in any kind of weather.

III.—Propelling Machinery, &c.

The "Olympic" and "Titanic" are triple screw steamers, having, as is well known, a combination of reciprocating engines with a low-pressure turbine. Great interest was manifested when this was announced, although it had been generally suspected that the success of the experiment in the White Star Canadian Liner "Laurentic"—which was the first large passenger steamer designed with this system of propulsion—would lead to the adoption of the same principle in the new vessels.

This arrangement of machinery is an advantage to the passengers, securing for them the utmost comfort by the smooth working of the ship. It is also the most satisfactory from an engineering point of view. The reciprocating engines exhaust into the low-pressure turbine, which drives the central propeller; the reciprocating engines, which drive the wing propellers, being sufficient for manœuvring in and out of port and going astern, so that there is no necessity for an astern turbine, which is required in steamers fitted with turbines only.

Steam Generating Plant.

There are twenty-nine boilers in the ship, having in all 159 furnaces. All of the boilers are 15' 9" in diameter; but twenty-four are double ended, being 20 feet long, while five are single-ended, being 11' 9" long. The shells of the latter are formed by one plate; the others have, as usual, three strakes. At each end there are three furnaces, all of the Morison type, with an inside diameter of 3′ 9″.   The working pressure is 215 lbs., and this, it is anticipated, will be maintained under natural draught conditions.   A view of the range of the boilers in Messrs. Harland & Wolff's works is given.   The boilers are arranged in six water-tight compartments, and owing to the great width of the ship it has been found possible to fit five boilers athwartship.   The boiler compartment nearest the machinery space accommodates the single-ended boilers, and these are so arranged as to be available for running the auxiliary machinery while the ship is in port, as well as for the general steam supply when the ship is at sea.   At the same time, two boilers in each of two other compartments have separate steam leads to the auxiliary machinery, which includes, of course, the electric-lighting installation—a considerable item in this vessel, as the total electric output is 1,600 kilowatts.   The other five rooms are fitted with the double-ended boilers, but owing to the fining of the ship, there are only four boilers in the forward room.   The four funnels are elliptical in plan, the dimensions being 24′ 6″ × 19′ 0″, and the average height above the level of the furnace bars is 150 feet.

The arrangements for the supply of fuel to the boilers are the result of great experience, and conceived with a view to minimising the amount of handling of the fuel for each boiler. There is a main bunker 'tween decks, immediately within the skin of the ship, and into this the coal will be first shipped, and subsequently distributed into bunkers athwart the ship and at the stokehold level.   These bunkers are arranged on each side of the main bulkheads, and therefore immediately in front of the furnaces ; so that each stoker practically takes his coal from the bunker-door.

In each of the five large boiler-rooms there are two See's ash-ejectors, and in addition there are four of Messrs. Railton & Campbell's ash-hoists for use when the vessels are in port. A large duplex pump of Harland & Wolff's own make is accommodated in a separate room in each boiler-room, the advantage being that the working parts of the pumps are not injuriously affected by dust. This pump works the ash-ejectors, circulates or feeds the boilers as required, and can also be used for pumping the bilges, except in three of the boiler rooms, where there are independent ballast pumps. In this way any of the six boiler compartments can be isolated, the pumps being independent so far as the inrush of sea-water is concerned. The pumps in each case are directly connected to the bilge, as well as to the general bilge system. The air is supplied to the stokeholds by electrically-driven "Sirocco" fans, of which there are twelve—two for each boiler-room.

General Arrangement of the Machinery.

A feature of the general arrangement of the combination machinery in this case is that, in view of the size of the units, the exhaust turbine, instead of being in the same engine-room with the two sets of piston engines, as in earlier ships, is accommodated in a separate compartment abaft the main reciprocating engine-room, and divided from it by a water-tight bulkhead.

In the reciprocating engine-room there are two sets of main engines—one driving the port and the other the starboard shaft; in the wings there are the main feed and hotwell, bilge,

sanitary, ballast, and fresh-water pumps, and a contact and surface heater; while on the port side a space has been found for the extensive refrigerating plant, instead of its being, as in some ships, far removed from the immediate observation of the engineers.

In the exhaust-turbine room there is fitted, immediately forward of the turbine, the manœuvring or change valves which control the flow of steam either to the turbine or to the condenser—the latter for manœuvring. This control, however, is exercised from the main starting platform through a Brown's engine of the hydraulic type, placed between the two change valves on the bulkhead. There is also here a steam-strainer, through which the steam passes on its way from the piston engines to the turbine in each wing. In this compartment there are placed the main condensers, together with their circulating pumps, twin air pumps, etc., evaporators and distilling plant, and forced lubrication pumps. There are also two pumps that can be used for bilge purposes, and a pump to take the hot salt water from the discharge pipe of the main condenser and send it to a tank at the top of the ship, for supplying the baths. There are two oil-coolers, and a pump for circulating the oil in them.

Abaft the exhaust turbine room and located on each side of the shaft driven by the turbine, and within the wing shafts, there are four sets of electric light engines. In addition to these engines there are placed, on a gallery well above the water-line in the exhaust turbine room, the two electric emergency sets. Steam pipes are led from three of the boiler-rooms to these emergency electric generators independently and above the watertight bulkheads. From this steam supply also it is possible to work any of the pumps connected to the bilges throughout the ship.

Boilers.

After end of Starboard Engine

Port Intermediate Cylinder,
Reciprocating Engine.

One of the Crank Shafts,
Reciprocating Engine.

Reciprocating Engines.

In these vessels the two sets of reciprocating engines—one driving each wing shaft—are of the four-crank triple type, arranged to work at 215 lbs. per square inch, and to exhaust at a pressure of about 9 lbs. absolute. These engines are on the "balanced" principle, and in their general design conform with the long-tried practice of Messrs. Harland & Wolff, Ltd. The high-pressure cylinder is 54 inches in diameter; intermediate cylinder 84 inches, and each of the two low-pressure cylinders 97 inches in diameter, the stroke being 75 inches in all cases. The sequence of valves and cylinders is as follows, beginning at the forward end:—Two slide valves, each with two ports in a common chest, worked by two rods through crosshead to single links, low-pressure cylinder, high-pressure cylinder, a single piston valve, two piston valves similarly arranged to the twin slide valves, intermediate pressure cylinder, low-pressure cylinder, and, finally, at the aft end, two slide valves. The valves are operated by the Stephenson link motion. Views of the starboard engine and port intermediate cylinder are given on page 60.

Forced lubrication is fitted to all the plummer-blocks of the shafting, the oil gravitating from a tank placed high in the turbine engine-room casing to the bearings, at a pressure of about 20 lbs., and draining to tanks low down in the ship, whence it is pumped through a filter and cooler to the high-level supply tank. There is also a water service through the plummer-blocks.

The crank and thrust-shafts are 27 in. in diameter, the line-shaft $26\frac{1}{4}$ in., and the tail-shaft $28\frac{1}{2}$ in., and they are all hollow, the crank and thrust-shafts having a 9 in. hole, and the others a 12 in. The shafting in all cases was machined at the works at Belfast. A view of one of the crank-shafts is given on page 60, and thrust-shaft on page 64. There is a loose coupling on the tail-shaft, so that it can be withdrawn from the stern, which greatly facilitates repair. The propellers driven by the reciprocating engines have each a cast-steel boss and three bronze blades, the diameter being 23 ft. 6 in.; and when developing 15,000 indicated horse-power for each engine, the revolutions will be 75 per minute.

Exhaust-Steam Turbine.

The exhaust-steam turbine, by which the central screw will be driven, is of the Parsons type, built to take exhaust steam at about 9 lbs. absolute, and expand it down to 1 lb. absolute, the condensing plant (described later) having been designed to attain a vacuum of $28\frac{1}{2}$ in. (with the barometer at 30 in.), the temperature of circulating water being 55 deg. to 60 deg. Fahr. The rotor, which is built up in the usual way, of steel forgings, is 12 feet in diameter, and the blades range in length from 18 in. to $25\frac{1}{2}$ in., being built on the segmental principle, laced on wire through the blades and distance-pieces, at the roots, and with binding soldered on the edge as usual. The length of the rotor between the extreme edges of the first and last ring of blades is 13 ft. 8 in. The casing is of cast iron, and was manufactured at the Belfast works. The patterns for parts of the casing are shown on page 64, while one of the casing castings is shown on page 64. There is no astern turbine, as the centre shaft is put out of action when the ship is being manœuvred. The bearings, thrust, and governor, are of the ordinary type adopted in Parsons' turbines. The turbine can be rotated by electric motor, and the usual lifting gear for the upper half of the casing and the rotor is also actuated by electric motor. Views of the turbine are represented on page 68.

The rotor has a weight of about 130 tons, and the turbine complete weighs 420 tons. The turbine shaft is $20\frac{1}{2}$ in. in diameter, the tail shaft $22\frac{1}{2}$ in., each with a 10 in. hole bored through it. The propeller driven by the turbine is built solid, of manganese bronze, with four blades, the diameter being 16 ft. 6 in. It is designed to run at 165 revolutions per minute, when the power developed is 16,000 shaft horse-power. A view of the turbine-driven propeller is given on page 64..

Manoeuvring Gear.

Between the boilers and the main steam stop valve there is a steam separator. There are two main steam leads from the boiler-room, each terminating at the stop valve and separator, which are situated against the forward engine-room bulkhead. The stop valves, however, are connected by a crosspipe, with two shut-off valves, so that either steam lead can be utilised for supplying steam to both engines. The main stop valve is of the equilibrium double-beat type, and is operated by hand wheel and screw, from the starting platform, which is situated in the centre of the piston engine-room.

One of the Thrust Shafts, Reciprocating
Engine.

Pattern of portion of
Turbine Casing.

Turbine Casing.

Turbine-Driven Propeller.

Pattern of portion of Turbine
Casing.

The exhaust pipes from the low-pressure cylinders connecting with the change-valve are fitted with bellows joints, which consist of two discs with special steel rings, and with flanges to take the pipes. The form of the disc-plates enables any difference in length, due to expansion or contraction, to be taken up. In order to ensure absolutely airtight joints, all the pipes in proximity to the condenser are fitted with these bellows joints.

The change-valves for shutting off steam to the turbine and simultaneously opening it to the condenser direct, for manœuvring purposes, are of the piston type with a ring of special form. When the pistons of these valves are in their highest position, steam has a clear flow to the strainer and thence to the turbine; when the piston is lowered the connection to the strainer is closed, and that to the condenser is opened. A view of the change-valve casing showing the parts is given on page 68. The piston of each change-valve is suspended to a suitably mounted lever, the other ends of both of which are connected to one of Brown's engines of hydraulic type, adopted in reciprocating engine practice; this hydraulic engine is actuated from the starting platform in the reciprocating engine-room.

The eduction pipes from the turbine to the condensers are fitted with large sluice-valves, to be closed in the case of accident to the turbine, when the reciprocating engines would exhaust through the change-valve direct to the condensers. These sluice-valves are, of course, of enormous area, and the closing slides are in two pieces, worked together through worm and rack gear. These sluice-valves are actuated by electric motors.

Condensing and Boiler-Feed Plant.

The condensers are of a form which has been used for some time on all engines built by Messrs. Harland & Wolff, Ltd. They are of pear shape, and a view of one of them is given on page 68. As is usual with turbine condensers, the inlet is of the full length of the condenser, and is well stayed vertically by division plates. In line with these there are in the condenser corresponding division plates, which secure an equal distribution of steam over the whole of the condenser tube area. Moreover, the pear shape concentrates the tube surface at the point where the largest volume of steam is admitted — therefore, where it is most needed.

There are four sets of gun-metal circulating pumps, two for the port and two for the starboard condensers, wtih 29 in. inlet pipes and driven by compound engines of the firm's own make. For each condenser there are two sets of Weir's air pumps, of the "dual" type, both air and water barrels being 36 inches in diameter by 21 inches stroke. The water from each condenser passes into a feed tank, thence it drains into a control tank, from which the hot well pumps draw it, discharging it through the Weir's surface heater to a Weir's contact heater, placed high on the engine-room bulkhead. The surface heater takes the exhaust from the electric engines for heating the feed, while the contact heater utilises the exhaust from the other auxiliaries for the same purpose. The water from the contact heater gravitates to the main feed pumps. Of these there are two pairs on each side of the reciprocating engine-room; two pairs are sufficient to feed the whole of the boilers. The main feed pumps have a diameter of 14 in. by 28 in. stroke, and steam cylinders of 19 in. diameter. The feed pump system is so arranged that all the pumps are interchangeable as far as the feeding of the boilers is concerned.

Refrigerating Installation.

The duty of cooling the ship's provision rooms, which are of very elaborate character, insulated and fitted up in accordance with the standard requirements of the White Star Line, cooling drinking-water, which is supplied at a large number of different points throughout the first, second and third class accommodation, cooling wine and beer in the bars, also a number of cold lockers in the pantries, larders, etc., making ice, and also for cooling the cargo-beef chambers, is performed by two horizontal duplex CO_2 machines, each of which combines two complete units capable of independent working, so that actually four refrigerating units are provided.

The machines are of the Hall's standard type, the compressors being bored from solid blocks of high-carbon steel, the condenser coils being of solid-drawn copper contained in the base casting, each of which is divided into two casings. Each machine has its own steam surface condenser, brass circulating pump, and air and feed pumps; a duplex brass-ended water pump is also provided as a stand-by. The evaporators are correspondingly divided into four units, and are placed in an insulated recess above the machines at the orlop deck level, at which level the brine pumps—three in number, with interchangeable connections—are placed. The brine return tanks are placed at a higher level, immediately above the evaporators.

Turbine Rotor being Bladed.

Turbine Rotor and Shaft in Lathe being Turned.

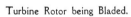

One of the Condensers.

Change Valve for Turbine Casing.

68

The brine circulation is on the open return system, with separate flow and return on each circuit. All brine pipes throughout are externally galvanized. The various circuits are of moderate length, and are interlaced in the chambers to ensure even distribution of the cooling effect, even in the remote contingency of one section becoming blocked.

Electric Lighting Plant.

For generating electric current for light and power, four 400 kilowatt engines and dynamos are fitted in a separate watertight compartment aft of the turbine room at tank top level. The engines, which indicate each about 580 horse power, are of the Allen vertical three-crank compound, enclosed forced lubrication type, running at 325 revolutions per minute. Each set has one high-pressure cylinder, 17 in. in diameter, and two low-pressure cylinders, each 20 in. in diameter, with a 13 in. stroke. They take steam at 185 lbs. pressure per square inch. The engines exhaust either into a surface heater—which is the usual seagoing condition—or to the condenser. Each engine is direct-coupled to a compound-wound continuous current dynamo, with an output of 100 volts and 4,000 amperes, so that their collective capacity is 16,000 amperes. The dynamos are of the ten-pole type, and are fitted with inter-poles.

In addition to the four main generating sets there are two 30-kilowatt engines and dynamos, placed in a recess off the turbine-room at saloon-deck level. Three sets can be supplied with steam from either of several boiler rooms, and will be available for emergency purposes. They are of a similar description to the main sets, but the engines are of the two-crank type.

The distribution of current is effected on the single wire system, and is controlled and metred at a main switchboard placed on a gallery in the electric engine-room, to which the main dynamo cables and feeders are connected. The latter pass up through port and starboard cable trunks to the various decks, radiating from thence to master switch and fuse boxes grouped at convenient points in the machinery spaces and accommodation, from whence run branches to the distribution fuse boxes scattered throughout the vessel, controlling the lamps and motors.

A complete system of electric lighting is, of course, provided, and electricity is also largely employed for heating, as well as for motive power, including no fewer than 75 motor-driven "Sirocco" fans from 55 in. to 20 in. in diameter, for ventilating all the passenger and crew spaces, as well as the engine and boiler rooms. All fan motors are provided with automatic and hand speed regulation.

Conclusion.

In the foregoing description the aim has been to convey to both the technical and the general reader some comprehensive idea of these steamers; but it would require a more voluminous work to do full justice to the subject.

The "Olympic" and "Titanic" are not only the largest vessels in the World; they represent the highest attainments in Naval Architecture and Marine Engineering; they stand for the pre-eminence of the Anglo-Saxon race on the Ocean; for the "Command of the Seas" is fast changing from a Naval to a Mercantile idea, and the strength of a maritime race is represented more by its instruments of commerce and less by its weapons of destruction than was formerly supposed. Consequently, these two Leviathans add enormously to the potential prosperity and progress of the race, and the White Star Line have well deserved the encomiums that have been showered upon them for their enterprise and foresight in the production of such magnificent vessels.

It is safe to predict that the "Olympic" and "Titanic" will enhance the great reputation already enjoyed by the Line; they are without a peer on the ocean; though so large, they are beautiful, alike in their appearance and in the simplicity of the working arrangements. Everything on board has been well—in many cases brilliantly—conceived and admirably carried out, and passengers will find comfort, luxury, recreation and health in the palatial apartments, the splendid Promenades, the Gymnasium, the Squash Racquet Court, the Turkish Baths, the Swimming Pond, Palm Court Verandah, etc. Moreover, the Staterooms, in their situation, spaciousness and appointments, will be perfect havens of retreat where many pleasant hours are spent, and where the time given to slumber and rest will be free from noise or other disturbance. Comfort, elegance, security—these are the qualities that appeal to passengers, and in the "Olympic" and "Titanic" they abound.

The horse has been described as the noblest work of the Creator; a ship may be said to be one of the finest of man's creations; and certainly the "Olympic" and "Titanic" deserve special recognition as the product of man's genius and enterprise. A ship—if the Ark can be so designated—played an important part in the early stage of man's development. To-day ships are amongst the greatest civilizing agencies of the age, and the White Star Liners "Olympic" and "Titanic"—eloquent testimonies to the progress of mankind, as shown in the conquest of mind over matter—will rank high in the achievements of the 20th century.